Right and Wrong and Being Strong

A Kid's Guide

Written by
Lisa O. Engelhardt

Illustrated by
R. W. Alley

ONE
CARING
PLACE

Abbey Press
St. Meinrad, IN 47577

For Ted, Jeff, and Laura

Text © 2001 Lisa O. Engelhardt
Illustrations © 2001 St. Meinrad Archabbey
Published by One Caring Place
Abbey Press
St. Meinrad, Indiana 47577

Library of Congress Catalog Number
00-109614

ISBN 978-0-87029-352-8

A Message to Parents, Teachers, and Other Caring Adults

Kids are works in progress. They aren't born knowing right from wrong. Somehow, over the years, we hope to guide them to become respectful, responsible adults.

In order to instill a healthy sense of right and wrong in children, we need to understand that they go through several stages of moral development. Very young children tend to believe, "Whatever I want is fair." They can learn to do what's right, though, to please adults and stay out of trouble. Early-elementary children consider, "What's in it for me?" They may begin to embrace the concept of "Do unto others"—mainly because they believe in rigid fairness. Kids in mid-to-upper elementary grades begin to guide their actions by social approval. High-schoolers finally start to achieve a sense of self-respect and respect for keeping the "system" working smoothly. Ideally, children evolve into grown-ups who can judge various life situations according to a well-informed moral sense of right and wrong.

While we can't necessarily control when and how children will move through each stage of moral development, we can steer them in the right direction. Families and classrooms can focus on a few, firm, clear rules, with immediate and consistent consequences. Adults also need to catch kids in the act of doing right—sharing, empathizing, using good judgment—and praise them for it. Most important of all, we need to be aware of the messages our own actions are sending.

Yes, children will take a zigzag course toward moral virtue (some more than others), but the set of values handed down to them will be the anchor that holds them steady, especially during the turbulent teens. Guided by our own moral convictions, and with generous helpings of patience and persistence, we can give our children a solid sense of right and wrong. May this little book open the door to healthy, helpful discussion between you and the children in your care.

—*Lisa O. Engelhardt*

Right and Wrong, Win and Lose

If you have ever watched a game show, you already know something about "right" and "wrong." The player who answers wrong loses the game. The player who answers right wins.

"Right" and "wrong" in life is a little bit like that. When you do a wrong thing, somebody loses—you or someone else. When you do the right thing, everybody wins.

If you grab the joystick away from your brother, he loses his spot at the computer. *You* lose something, too—the chance to be fair and kind. But what if you take turns or play a game together? Then you *both* win!

Here's another way to look at it. What if everybody in the whole world did this thing? For example, what if everybody in every restaurant in the world shot paper wads out of their straws. Would the world be better or worse?

Telling Right From Wrong

Probably the simplest way to tell right from wrong is to ask yourself: Will this hurt someone, maybe even myself? Will it hurt someone's feelings or things? If so, then it's the wrong thing to do.

If a girl kicks you on the school bus, it's wrong to kick her back, because it would hurt her. (You know this, because it hurt when she kicked *you*!)

What if you tore her notebook to get back at her? Wrong—because you would hurt something that belongs to her.

What if you said, "I don't like being kicked—please don't do it anymore"? Right! This helps to stop the problem without hurting anyone or anything.

Obeying the Rules

You have rules in your home and classroom to help you to know what's right and wrong. If you disobey those rules, there will be some kind of penalty, like a time-out or an early bedtime.

But what if you do something wrong and don't get caught? Let's say you eat some junk food right before dinnertime—and nobody sees you. Does that make it okay?

No. Just because you "get away" with something does not mean it's right. You have still hurt somebody. In this case, you have hurt *yourself*, by spoiling your appetite.

Doing Right

We want to do the right thing because we don't want to hurt anyone. We want to treat others the way *we* would like to be treated.

The holy writings of every faith talk about how to be a good and loving person. They tell us to help others, be kind, share, and forgive.

They also tell us that God loves every single one of us. God wants us to love each other. If we hurt someone else, or ourselves, we hurt God. When we do something wrong, it's like turning our back on God.

Your Conscience

You may have seen cartoons where someone is trying to make a decision. A little angel stands on one shoulder, telling the person to do the right thing. A little devil stands on the other shoulder, telling the person to do the wrong thing.

That doesn't happen in real life, of course. But your "conscience" is a little bit like that angel. Your conscience is a feeling inside of you that helps you to do the right thing.

When you do something wrong, it might "bother" your conscience. You may feel guilty or ashamed, and wish you hadn't done it.

Everybody Makes Mistakes

If you've hurt someone by doing something wrong, admit it and say you're sorry.

Try to think of a way to make that person feel better. Could you draw a picture to show how sorry you are? Could you fix what you've broken or return what you've taken?

God knows that everyone makes mistakes. And God knows when you're truly sorry. Ask God to forgive you and help you to do better the next time.

Good and Bad Days

Do you ever feel like you're having a bad day? Maybe you're tired and crabby. Maybe your sister is bugging you. Maybe you really want to do something that you're not allowed to do.

You can't help the way you *feel*. But you *can* help the way you *act*. You don't *have* to be mean when you're mad. You don't *have* to yell at your sister when she's being bratty. You don't *have* to use your dad's cool new drill without asking.

YOU are in control of your mouth and hands and feet. You have the power to do what's right. You can't change other people or control what they do. But you *can* control your own actions.

Lying, Cheating, and Stealing

If you lie and say your cousin broke the lamp, when you did it, you hurt your cousin because he gets the blame. But you also hurt yourself. If you get into a habit of lying, people learn not to trust you anymore.

If you have "brain lock" on a test and peek at a classmate's paper, you hurt yourself too. The teacher won't know that you need help with that lesson, and then you might have trouble with later lessons.

What if you steal a pack of trading cards? This hurts the store owner, who needs to sell things to make money. It might also hurt your conscience, because you know stealing is not right.

Going Along to Belong

Sometimes kids think that in order to be liked, they have to be just like other kids. It's normal to want to fit in with the group. But you're headed for trouble if you think you have to go along with something wrong to belong.

What if your friends invite you to come along with them and soap the windows of the crabby man down the street? You know it's not right to mess up someone's house, but you don't want your friends to think you're chicken.

BE TRUE TO YOU—and to your own sense of right and wrong. Friends who want you to do something wrong aren't really friends at all. You can suggest something else to do, or just say, "No thanks," and walk away.

Drugs and Drinking

Taking drugs not ordered by your doctor, and drinking beer or whiskey before you are old enough is against the law.

They are wrong because they can hurt you. They can make your brain act strangely, so that you can't think straight or move right. They can cause very bad problems in your body.

Sometimes older kids think it's cool to try out drinking or drugs. DON'T DO IT! You're not being cool; you're being a fool to put something in your body that is bad for you.

Violence

You may have seen video games where you get points for hitting or kicking the "bad guy." Games like this give kids the wrong message, because "violence" (trying to hurt other people) is wrong.

In some very rare cases, where their own lives are in danger, people need to fight back. This is called "self-defense," and it is the only time when it makes sense to hurt someone else.

When you are having a disagreement with someone, you have other choices besides fighting. You can talk or walk. It's not right to fight. Use your personal power for peace.

Being and Doing Good

Being good isn't just about what NOT TO DO. It's also about what TO DO.

It's *right* not to soap the neighbor's windows. But it's *good* to help him carry in his groceries. It's *right* not to call other kids names. It's *good* to invite them to play.

It's good to help people who are not being treated fairly. This is especially true if they cannot stand up for themselves for some reason—maybe because they are too shy, for example.

It's not enough just to go along with the rules. Go beyond the rules—to help, to give, to stand up for, to do good.

Feeling Confused

Some things are not clearly right *or* wrong. For example, is it right or wrong for you to quit piano lessons? It might help you to have more free time. But it might hurt you, if you wish later that you had stuck with it.

Try listing all the GOOD things and BAD things that might happen if you make a certain choice. It may all become clearer written down on paper.

It also helps to pray. God always wants only the best for you. Ask God to guide you in making the right choice.

A Better World

Just listen to the news, and you can tell there's a lot of wrong going on in the world. But you can help to make the world better, little by little.

Every time you don't get back at someone who hurt you, you make the world a more peaceful place. Every time you stand up for others' rights, you make the world a fairer place. Every time you choose right instead of wrong, you make the world a better place.

The most important thing to remember is to do the loving thing. Do that...and you'll never go wrong!

Lisa O. Engelhardt is the editorial director for Abbey Press, the author of 12 gift and children's books, and a freelance giftware writer for WordSpring. She has also written several adult Elf-help books for Abbey Press.

R. W. Alley is the illustrator for the popular Abbey Press adult series of Elf-help books, as well as an illustrator and writer of children's books. He lives in Barrington, Rhode Island, with his wife, daughter, and son. See a wide variety of his works at: www.rwalley.com.